THIRD PRINTING

GATES & fences

STRAIGHT TALK IN A CROOKED WORLD

Lori Wagner

Discovering the Blessings of Biblical Boundaries

Gates & Fences: Straight Talk in a Crooked World
Copyright © 2006 by Lori Wagner

ISBN: 978-0-97986-270-0

Library of Congress Control Number: 2007905933

Scripture quotations are from the King James Version (KJV) and the New
International Version (NIV) © 1973, 1978, 1984, International Bible Society,
unless otherwise indicated.

Requests for information should be addressed to:
· Affirming Faith
1181 Whispering Knoll Lane
Rochester Hills, MI 48306
loriwagner@affirmingfaith.com
www.affirmingfaith.com

Cover design and photography by Christina Harper
www.cmhphotography.com

Printed in the United States of America.

REVIEWS

Lori Wagner takes a vital stand and encourages us to join her. She tackles the issues that face Christians of all ages firmly and biblically with a clarity that cannot be ignored nor lightly dismissed. This book is an expression of deep concern about a widespread undermining of the authority of Scripture concerning moral purity and holiness. Thank you Lori, I applaud you for taking the time to write on these all important and timely issues. This book is a must read for all ages.

Gwyn Oakes
Ladies Ministries President, UPCI

Lori Wagner both inspires and convicts me personally with this offering. This work is both creative and targeted to "gates" all must go through on the journey to and in adult life. She offers spiritual wisdom through the "fences" examined. Her tone reaches out as one who cares for those traveling through necessary paths while offering help that will truly impact through the years yet to come.

Lisa Crump
National Coordinator Manager, National Day of Prayer Task Force

This book is a succinct powerhouse of practical wisdom for youth of all ages! I will be able to recommend it to my pastoral peers with joy! What you have provided for young people will be a gate to a godly future and a fence to ward off distractions, deceptions and spiritual destruction. Thank you for allowing God to use you to author 21st Century insight into His everlasting principles.

Rev. Marvin Walker
Pastor, Faith Apostolic Church of Troy

YPA'! (oora! hurrah!) A word that comes from the Russian language. Lori Wagner's new book is just that ... YPA'! It is refreshing, exciting and graced with great clarity. Lori has "pushed the spiritual envelope" and declared God's great Word again, for New Spiritual wineskins. In touching our faith, and God's infallible Word, Lori Wagner reinforces that which has been written and said ... God loves us deeply and devotedly, so He is not afraid to say, "NO." A work of deep insight and practical living.

Rev. G.L. Linville
Pastor and Author of "Man in Mid-Life Crisis"

I am always looking for something that is able to express even more God's plan for our lives. This book does that in a practical and anointed way. Well written and interesting, this book will enhance anyone's walk with God.

Donna Linville
Pastor's Wife and International Speaker

What an awesome book! If I was still a youth leader, I would get one for every teen. Thank you, Lori! I wish more adults were as bold and caring as you in ministry. I will share this book with as many as God will allow me to, so we can get the good word out that good fences make not only good neighbors, but good and righteous children in the Kingdom of Heaven!

Bernie Lutchman
Communications Director, Businessmen in Christ

I wish I had this when I was raising my son. I would recommend this book for every parent. It is so enlightening, and yet written so a "spoonful of sugar helps the medicine go down!"

Claudette Walker
International Ladies Conference Speaker

I love it! Your book is perfect inspiration to rise above the culture's view of sexuality for teens and is entirely consistent with the message we are trying to teach from the home front. It's great to "see it in print" from an outside source. It was easy to hand your book over to my teen daughter, and it helped both of us clearly articulate things that we don't often hear in our culture.

Christine Gibson
Editor of "Mom's, Inc.," Newsletter

Wandering in an unforgiving wasteland, bereft of constants, hungry, thirsty and cold, this generation is in desperate need of a wise friend -- one who's been there and knows the way home. Into the middle of the need comes "Gates & Fences" bringing new understanding to words like closure and parameters. If you're an adult, read it and weep for your children and their children too, then give copies to every young person you know. If you're a young person, read it and thank God for the voice of experience, which is illuminating the plain path and saying, "This is the way, walk in it." Then, when you've absorbed it, share your copy with any and every one you consider to be a friend. You'll be doing them a truly great favor.

Marjorie Kinnee
Author and Managing Editor of "The Apostolic Writers' Digest"

$\mathscr{D}$

This book was written for Christian singles and young people everywhere in hopes of inspiring them to live morally excellent lives.

Specifically, I dedicate these writings to my precious family with gratitude for their love and support:

To my husband Bill. Thanks for believing in me and supporting me in every way imaginable.

To our children, Ashley, Noelle, Charles and Hope. My greatest desire is to see you walk in Truth because you love Jesus.

CONTENTS

ACKNOWLEDGMENTS

I would like to acknowledge the kind and expert assistance of my editor, Marjorie Kinnee. Her wisdom and experience have been invaluable to me.

Thank you to my sister, Christina Harper, for providing beautiful visual examples of gates and fences for the cover and many of the chapters. Thank you also for your affirming words that prodded me to explore the "gates and fences" in this book.

Thank you Pastor and Mrs. Marvin Walker and my church family at Faith Apostolic Church of Troy. Your support has meant so much.

Thank you, my ladies prayer partners, for years of sustaining prayers, comfort and encouragement, and especially my dearest friends Carolyn McKenzie, Patty Dourjalian and Lisa Riley who hug me or kick me as needed.

Thank you, Barb Dyrdul, for faithfully speaking into my life and pushing me out of my box, encouraging me to dream big for Jesus.

Thank you to the kind people who reviewed the content of *Gates and Fences* and told me it was worth pursuing.

And most of all I thank you, Jesus, for Your Word and the way You open it to Your people in new ways giving fresh insight and enabling us to share precious truths with others.

INTRODUCTION

Almost ten years ago the Lord impressed me to write a book about gates. Having no experience developing and composing a full-length manuscript, I was clueless how to even begin such an undertaking. Oh, I tried off and on over the years. I would drag out my concordance, study the Bible, research online and try to make it happen. I even carried a level of guilt that I wasn't doing what I had been assigned to do -- but it wasn't the right time.

The Bible says "there is a time for every purpose under heaven." I realize now that before I was able to begin this project, I first had to live through the previous decade gaining understanding, sitting under good teaching and experiencing life with teenagers. After ten years, the time was right. In one short hour the Lord revealed what the gates and fences were, an introduction was written, and ten chapter titles were developed.

After months of work, the task is now complete. It's my prayer that as you read, you will be encouraged as we explore the sturdy and reliable fences of protection our loving Father has placed around our lives. God wants what's best for us, and His plans are better than anything we could come up with on our own. He always has our best interest at heart. If we can accept that, we will be on the right path to understanding the blessings of Biblical boundaries.

The Lord's guidelines are more than "good" fences. They are "God" fences that keep us from falling prey to the very real attempts of our spiritual adversary to separate us from the beautiful plans God has for our lives.

3

1

LIFE INSIDE THE GATES AND FENCES

The Blessings of Biblical Boundaries

We're Christians. If God Almighty says "no," that should be the end of the discussion … right? But something in us wants to know the whys. Why should a young single Christian adhere to old-fashioned, irrelevant concepts like purity or modesty? Why should people respect those in authority over them? Why wait for marriage to experience the pleasure of our God-given gift of sexuality?

In our world today, godly virtues are not simply ignored, they are mocked. Television shows ridicule people with Biblical convictions. Magazine covers and billboards feature models more nude than clothed. But although society continues its moral downward spiral, God's Word remains unchanged.

When Jesus taught, He often used parables to relay spiritual principles in ways His followers could understand. In our world today, God still uses natural examples to give His people insight into spiritual matters.

In the spiritual world, there are also gates and fences that define our boundaries and provide structure and security for our lives.

All across the country, we see gates and fences of all sizes and shapes. In the spiritual world, there are also gates and fences that define our boundaries and provide structure and security for our lives. Although we can't see them, they are there. Understanding that Biblical "fences" were established by God for our benefit enables us to live more peacefully within their protection.

✍

Every year in high school classrooms across America students study Robert Frost's famous poem "Mending Wall." The composition examines several questions: Why do good fences make good neighbors? What is the purpose of a wall anyway? What is being walled in? What is being walled out?

In his poem, Frost examines how a strong, accurate fence benefits the relationship between two neighbors. Applying this concept spiritually, we understand the unseen "fences" (or boundaries) set by God were established for the good of His people. Strong, true spiritual fences benefit our relationships both in the natural and the spiritual.

The Word reveals that our lives and our bodies do not belong to us, but to God. They were purchased through the cross of Jesus Christ, and He has the authority to draw our boundary lines. As the servants of God, we join the company of many great people who have also been called His servants: Moses (Deuteronomy 34:5), the Apostle Paul (Romans 1:1), King David (II Samuel 3:18), and Joshua (Joshua 24:29).

During the time of Jesus' earthly ministry, an estimated half of all people in the Roman world were slaves or bond servants. These were prisoners of war or the poor and indebted who actually sold themselves into slavery. When they did this, they voluntarily chose to forfeit their rights and became the literal possessions of their masters.

Today every Christian believer is the possession of God (I Corinthians 7:22, Ephesians 6:6) – not because God wants to prove His power and superiority, but because He knew our great need of redemption. Being bonded to Christ means we release our rights to control our own lives in exchange for our salvation and the joy of serving the one true and living God, the King of Kings and Lord of Lords! This is a high honor and privilege, and the rewards are not only great, but eternally wonderful!

The Lord's guidelines are more than "good" fences. They are "God" fences that keep us from falling prey to the very real attempts of our spiritual adversary to separate us from the beautiful plans God has for our lives.

Jeremiah 29:11 assures us God's plans are for our good – to give us hope and a future. We like all the good parts of God's plans, like being overcomers and having eternal life, but living with boundaries doesn't sound like much fun. Why can't we live by the 70s motto, "If it feels good, do it"?

Robert Frost understood man's struggle and expressed it well when he wrote "Something there is that doesn't love a wall, that wants it down." Our natural response is to want the walls down. But is that what's best in the long run?

In the coming chapters, we'll examine some fences and gates in great detail. Hold on to your hats as we explore some controversial and delicate subjects.

$\mathscr{L}$

Jesus, help me approach the subject of Biblical boundaries with an open mind, understanding that You have far more insight and wisdom than I have. Your Word reveals that Your purposes and plans are for my good, even when I don't understand them. Give me a heart that seeks to please You and reveal my love for You by following Your commandments and instructions.

CHAPTER REVIEW AND APPLICATION

The major theme of this chapter is:

_____

_____

How are godly values portrayed in the media today?

_____

_____

What is your attitude towards Biblical boundaries (rules)?

_____

_____

Taking a moment for an honest evaluation, analyze the following questions: Are your values more in line with secular society's or God's Word?

_____

_____

_____

Are the choices you make and your reactions to Biblical boundaries evident as nonbelievers observe your Christian walk?

_____

_____

_____

As a believer, what does the Bible say about who should have control over your life and for what reason?

_____

_____

Why would a loving Father establish guidelines for his children?

_____

_____

Through God's help, what types of improvements would you like to make in your attitude towards Biblical restrictions?

_____

_____

As you purpose to please God by honoring and respecting the guidelines He put forth for you in His Word, take a moment to write your personal prayer to Him.

_____

_____

_____

_____

_____

_____

_____

_____

_____

_____

_____

_____

... there are spiritual umbrellas protecting us in the supernatural realm. These coverings are constructed of those in authority over our lives – those responsible for our spiritual well being. We protect our souls when we respectfully submit to their care and instructions.

11

2

GOTCHA COVERED

The Fence of Submission to Authority

The first and most important section of our spiritual gates and fences is the vital area of submitting to authority. I know, we don't really want to go here, but we would be wasting our time with chapters 3-13 if we didn't. Respecting authority is not merely a fence in itself. It's more like the concrete footings poured around the base of the fence posts keeping them securely in the ground. So, here we go …

As believers, we like to hear about the protection of God. That makes us feel safe. Everyone wants to feel sheltered from the storms of life or the threat of enemy attack. But do we have any obligation to God in order to receive His divine protection? Or is He that sweet, loving, "Sugar Daddy" in the sky just waiting to pour out blessings on us, His beloved children?

We appreciate verses like James 4:7b " ... *Resist the devil and he will flee from you.* " But, we have to take Scripture in the context it was written, and the first part of this verse instructs: *"Submit yourselves therefore to God ..."* **To have the authority and power to resist satan, we must *first* be submitted to God.**

THE CONCEPT OF SPIRITUAL COVERING

Picture yourself out in a storm. It's raining cats and dogs, but you are safe and dry under a big umbrella. Now, you have a choice. You can choose to stay dry beneath the umbrella's protection or step outside the covering. If you do, however, there will be consequences. You will expose yourself to the physical elements and definitely get soaked by the rain.

In the same way, there are spiritual umbrellas protecting us in the supernatural realm. These coverings are constructed of those in authority over our lives – those responsible for our spiritual well being. We protect our souls when we respectfully submit to their care and instruction.

An important aspect of submitting to God is respecting and obeying the authority He established. Jude 1:8 tells us that <u>ungodly people reject authority</u>, but honoring authority is one primary way Christians demonstrate their respect for God to the world. Acts 23:5 instructs believers to refrain from speaking evil of rulers. Romans 13:1 says *"Let every person be in subjection to the governing authorities."*

Here are some additional verses on the subject:

Submit yourselves for the Lord's sake to every authority instituted among men: whether to the king, as the supreme authority, or to governors ... (I Peter 2:13-14 NIV)

Remind the people to be subject to rulers and authorities, to be obedient, to be ready to do whatever is good.
(Titus 3:1 NIV)

In I Timothy 2:1-2, Paul exhorts us to pray *"for kings and all who are in authority."*

It's our choice. It's up to us to remain under the spiritual covering of those who have authority over us. For young and unmarried people, the first level of authority is their parents/guardians. Pastors come next, and they all come under God's authority. We will NOT be protected by God if we are out from under the covering of our pastor or parents. It just doesn't work that way.

Here's the real kicker. Submission isn't really submission until you reach a point of disagreement. My husband and I have absolutely no problems in the area of Biblical authority – that is, as long as he's doing everything I want. But that's not really living under authority, is it?

Search your memory banks and see if you can recall a television show made in this decade where the father or authority figure is an intelligent, respectable person. What about ministers? They are portrayed as narrow-minded, bumbling idiots. Sit-coms in particular almost always depict men as feebleminded and controlled by strong, intelligent women. But kids really rule the roost, going behind parents' backs lying and manipulating to get around established guidelines. Sadly, these shows are far more than simple comedies. They are broadcast documentaries on the skewed relationships in homes across America.

This is not God's plan. He is a God of order, and He has established the principle of authority so we can live in peace. Think about the old saying, "Too many chiefs and not enough Indians." We need leadership – a "pecking order" if you want to call it that – to define our roles at home, church, the workplace and in the community. Yes, the "buck" has to stop somewhere … and I'm glad it's not me! I would prefer not to have to carry the tremendous burdens and responsibilities of those in higher levels of authority and decision making.

One very powerful lesson on respecting authority is revealed in Genesis 16:1-10. The Lord spoke directly to Hagar telling her to return to her mistress and submit herself *"under her hand."* That was not an easy thing. Sarai, her mistress, was being unfair. Even so, Hagar obeyed God's instructions in her very difficult situation, and through her obedience, she and her son gained God's protection and provision.

The principle of authority also applies to teachers, bosses, public servants, etc. Hebrews 13:17 says to obey them that have the rule over you. This specifically refers to those who are over us spiritually, but the Bible also tells believers to be obedient to civil authority. We are to pay our taxes (Mark 12:17) and *"be subject unto the higher powers"* (Romans 13:1-7).

God and His Word are One, so when we are obedient to the written Word, we are submitting to God Himself. The Ten Commandments aren't the Ten Suggestions. The Golden Rule isn't the Golden Idea. When we live according to Biblical instruction the blessings of God will come into our lives. Even those who don't serve God are still blessed when they follow Scriptural guidelines.

An experiment was conducted at a school playground. The administration thought the playground fences were restricting the children, so they took them down. Prior to this, the children played safely throughout the entire playground, but after the fences were removed, they huddled in the middle of the playground afraid to venture out. The fences had promoted feelings of safety that permitted the children to relax and enjoy themselves without feeling threatened by outside elements.

When we know where the fences are, we can live freely within their security. When the fences aren't defined, the result is instability and insecurity.

> *When we know where the fences are, we can live freely within their security. When the fences aren't defined, the result is instability and insecurity.*

One word of caution, however: we must have confidence that our leadership is taking us in the right direction. Paul said in I Corinthians 11:1, *"Be ye followers of me, even as I also am of Christ."* The things we are asked to do should be backed up by the Word. It's not wrong to ask for clarification if we don't understand, as long as we keep a respectful attitude and make sure we are doing so at an appropriate time and place. We don't want to be caught wearing the "emperor's new clothes" blindly following the counsel of one in error. However, most pastors truly seek the wisdom of God in leading their congregations, and they deserve our honor and respect.

Lord Jesus, please help me submit with a right spirit to the authority you established in my life. It makes sense when I think about a toddler obeying his mom and dad who care for him and protect him, but it's sometimes hard to accept instructions as I mature and want to make my own decisions. Help me realize that the people you placed over me care deeply for me and have more experience, knowledge and wisdom than I have at this stage in my life. Cause me to remember this: instead of bucking against those in authority over me, I should lift them to You in prayer. Thank You for covering me with Your divine protection as I follow in Your Word and honor Your ways.

CHAPTER REVIEW AND APPLICATION

The major theme of this chapter is:

_____

_____

Explain in your own words the blessings and protection of living according to the Biblical principle of spiritual covering.

_____

_____

_____

_____

Explain some potential results of choosing to live outside the covering of authority God placed in your life?

_____

_____

What does Jude 1:8 say about the reaction of ungodly people towards authority?

_____

_____

How does this apply to parents, pastors, teachers, civil servants?

_____

_____

_____

What can we learn from Hagar's example as she submitted to the authority of God in a difficult situation?

_____

_____

Explain what you learned by the playground experiment.

_____

_____

_____

As you purpose to please God by honoring and respecting the guidelines He put forth for you in His Word in the area of authority, take a moment to write your personal prayer to Him.

_____

_____

_____

_____

_____

_____

_____

_____

_____

_____

_____

*The relationships that are most important to us send
a loud message to both God and to the world about
the condition of our hearts.*

3

GOOD NEIGHBORS MAKE GOOD FENCES

The Fence of Godly Companionship

We've read how good fences make good neighbors, but let's also consider how good neighbors make good fences. Friendships impact our lives, and choosing godly friends cultivates a hedge of protection around our hearts and minds.

It's undeniable. Our friends influence us. We pick up each others' habits and sayings, our likes and dislikes. That can be great ... or it can be a cause for concern.

One Scripture deals directly with how hanging with the wrong crowd negatively impacts our character.

"Do not be misled: bad company corrupts good character."
(I Corinthians 15:33 NIV)

Define bad, you say? Well, take the following Scripture for example:

Do not make friends with a hot-tempered man, do not associate with one easily angered, or you may learn his ways and get yourself ensnared. (Proverbs 22:24-25 NIV)

If our friendships are with hot-tempered people, chances are great we will adopt their angry nature. The same holds true for complaining, gossiping, self-indulgent and worldly people. We absorb the nature of those we spend time with. The more time we spend with someone, the more of their nature we take on.

This is true in the negative, but it can be a very good thing, too. Just think, the more you are in the presence of God, the more you take on His very positive nature! And if we choose wise friends, their wisdom will rub off on us.

He who walks with wise men will be wise, But the companion of fools will be destroyed. (Proverbs 13:20)

If our friends influence us to sin or don't care about our relationship with God, we need to reevaluate those relationships. That is not true friendship. True friends will encourage you in your walk with God. They care enough to tell you the truth about the choices you make, even when they know you don't want to hear it!

If your friends poke fun at godly people, that's a big warning sign. If your friends are disobedient, envious, backbiting, argumentative or reject the Truth of the Word of God, that should send up a big red flag. Have you noticed that after being with someone like this you have negative feelings toward others you didn't have before? Has a relationship caused you to change or join in with the same type of negative talk?

God addresses the need for good relationships in the very first Psalm. He must think this is a pretty big deal. As you read Psalm 1, you'll see that God warns against walking in the counsel of the ungodly. We don't want to take their advice, because their thinking isn't based in Truth. Psalm 1 goes on to say that when we delight in the law of the Lord, we will prosper. This Scripture uses strong language to declare the ungodly will perish, but also promises God knows the path of the righteous.

Do you want to be known by God? He is the very best friend you will ever have. It's amazing the Creator of the universe is interested in having a friendship with us, but He is. Consider how God walked in the garden with Adam and Eve. He shared the cool of the day in their company simply because it gave Him pleasure.

Scripture tells us that Abraham was a *friend* of God. God confided His intimate thoughts and feelings with Abraham because they had a relationship built on trust and respect.

Kingdoms have fallen when rulers listened to evil people who presented themselves as friends. One example involves King David's son, Amnon. His story is told in II Chronicles 17-18.

Amnon was not a bad guy. He had a good upbringing, a great reputation, was well educated and had a good conscience … but he also had a "friend." That "friend" gave him poor counsel.

Amnon was in love, but had decided he should stay true to his principles, even though it broke his heart. When his "friend" Jonadab noticed he was down in the dumps, he gave Amnon some bad advice that resulted in the ruin of an innocent girl and the loss of Amnon's own life. In the end, Scripture indicates Jonadab was aware of the conspiracy resulting in Amnon's death. Some friend. It is crucial to be aware of the character and intent of those we allow to speak into our lives.

Instead of listening to the voices of those appealing to our carnal natures, we would do better to seek relationships with those concerned about our character and our future – those who will challenge us in our Christian walk to do more and be more for Jesus.

As iron sharpens iron, so one man sharpens another. (Proverbs 27:17 NIV)

Ask any drug addict, "Where did you get your first hit?" The answer will almost always be "from a friend." What about the alcoholic? Hey, a friend can get us hooked on lots of things – a TV show, paint ball, karaoke, scrapbooking, prayer – just about anything. So be careful and make sure all your closest friends are hooked on Jesus. That's a great common interest to share.

The relationships that are most important to us send a loud message to both God and the world about the condition of our hearts. You have probably heard the saying, "Birds of a feather flock together." We are naturally attracted to people who share our views, likes and dislikes. If we are rebellious, we attract rebellious people. If we are strong Christians, we attract other strong Christians. If we're lukewarm, we'll have lukewarm friends.

> *We're not supposed to scratch around on the ground with the turkeys ... we're supposed to soar with the eagles!*

We're not supposed to scratch around on the ground with the turkeys ... we're supposed to soar with the eagles!

And remember this, real friendship looks at the heart, not the external "packaging." Real friendship is based on honesty and trust. Scripture has a lot to say about friendship, but one of my favorite verses is:

A friend loveth at all times, and a brother is born for adversity.
(Proverbs 17:17)

Isn't it great to have friends, brothers and sisters in our lives? If your friends are Christian, they are also your brothers and sisters in Christ.

It's good to know we're not alone in this world. We can cover each others' backs and offer encouragement when it's needed. Thank God for true friends, brothers and sisters in the Lord, who impact our lives in so many positive ways.

Jesus, You are my best friend. I am amazed that You would love me enough to die for my sins. You are a true friend that never uses people for selfish motives. You are loving and kind, yet wise and firm in Your counsel. Your Word tells me to be cautious about the people I bring in to my "inner circle" of close friends. Please help me make good decisions. Help me trust my parents and godly leaders to guide me in my relationships. Give me discernment to see into the hearts of those around me. And Lord, please help me be a good friend to others and to You.

CHAPTER REVIEW AND APPLICATION

The major theme of this chapter is:

_____

_____

Explain how some of the friendships you have impact your life in negative and positive ways.

_____

_____

_____

_____

What does I Corinthians 15:33 say about our relationships?

_____

_____

What are some of the character traits exhibited by those we should <u>not</u> develop close relationships with?

_____

_____

What are some of the character traits exhibited by those we should
want to develop close relationships with?

_____

_____

Would you consider God to be your best friend? Why?

_____

_____

What message do you think your closest relationships convey to the
world about the condition of your heart?

_____

_____

_____

_____

As you purpose to please God by honoring and respecting the Word in the area of relationships, take a moment to write your personal prayer to Him.

_____

_____

_____

_____

_____

_____

_____

_____

_____

_____

_____

_____

Dressing sensually ... is taking a step away from purity and towards fulfilling provocative desires that steer us in the wrong direction. Modesty is a separation from worldliness and will, in fact, deter immorality in our lives.

4

MODEST IS HOTTEST!

The Fence of Modesty

We don't hear much about modesty in the world today. Currently acceptable styles of dress passed the threshold of decency long ago. However, the Word of God hasn't changed on the issue. God still values modesty. He established it as a fence of protection around us.

After Adam and Eve sinned, their eyes were opened to their nakedness. Once they realized this, Scripture tells us they made themselves "aprons" out of leaves. Get a picture in your mind of an apron. There are short ones that tie at the waist and those that have bibs covering the chest area as well. How much of the body does an apron cover, and how much does it leave exposed?

Now back to the Garden. Even with their new clothes on, Adam and Eve knew they weren't properly covered and hid themselves from God. God must have found their garments insufficient as well, because He created tunics (or robes) for them from the skins of the sacrifice offered for their sin. The clothes God made covered more than just their "private parts."

There are obviously a lot of different styles, but if the clothes we choose are more apron-like than robe- or tunic-like in the way they cover our bodies, perhaps we should reevaluate our wardrobes. What's the motive behind what we're wearing? Is our goal to please God or to feed our own base desires, like the lust of the flesh and the pride of life? Is the principle of modesty in our hearts?

When we come in contact with others, we communicate with them through many methods. We know about communicating with our eyes, ears and mouths, but we also send and receive messages with other body parts, whether they are openly exposed or not. You've probably heard the term "body language," but have you considered your "dressing language?" Are you classy ... flashy ... or trashy?

Whatever clothing you select, the focal point of your appearance should be your face. Isn't it your face you want people looking at ... not your sexuality on display?

I'm not advocating that Christians should wear sloppy, ill-fitting clothes. Modesty doesn't mean wearing a burlap bag. It's okay to be fashionable and well dressed, and it's quite possible for young women to be both modest and lovely to look at.

We are God's ambassadors to the world and should conduct ourselves with dignity. Keep in mind that fleeting runway trends, and even the weather, should not dictate more than the Word of God the styles and manner of dress we choose to put on our bodies. After all, we are the temple of the living God!

Before you go out the door, look in the mirror and ask yourself if God would go out in public wearing what you are wearing … because if you are a Christian, He is … in you!

My sister told me about a speaker who taught a seminar addressing what she calls the "no zone." This is the area of the body from the upper to lower torso where we shouldn't be touching one another. Would it be fair to extrapolate that **if others shouldn't be touching our "no zones" with their hands, why would we want them touching these personal areas with their eyes?** Makes sense, doesn't it?

To take it a step further, as a lady, I might pick a dress that covers me from neck to ankles, but if it is clingy or has a vacuum-sealed appearance, it's not modest. It's not drawing attention to my face. As a matter of fact, it's a form of sexual teasing.

Men are visually sensitive, and when a woman dresses immodestly, she entices the men around her to sin. Jesus said that if we entertain lustful thoughts we have committed adultery (Matthew 5:28). I wouldn't want to bear the guilt of causing others to sin. It's a sad situation when conscientious men are afraid to look at many women because they are dressed inappropriately. **When women are dressed modestly, men are free to enjoy their beauty without sexual temptation.** As a woman, I would prefer to be considered lovely to look at over sexually enticing.

Now I'm really going to step on some toes (I know, because I've talked to my teenagers about this). It is beyond my comprehension why a single young lady would wear sexy lingerie. In particular, thong panties (the uniform of topless dancers) and cleavage enhancing wonder bras promote feelings of sensuality a single person shouldn't be arousing in themselves or the people around them. What legitimate reason could a single person have for wearing these provocative items of clothing?

A young lady actually told me they thought it was good to wear thong underwear so people wouldn't see her panty lines. My friend, if this is your reason for wearing thong underwear, I have to say, "Your clothes are too tight!"

Even if no one ever sees our undergarments, what we wear under our clothing affects the way we feel about ourselves, and this transmits to those with whom we come in contact.

Arguing that undergarments aren't a factor in our attitudes doesn't hold water as far as I am concerned. Just think about it. What was the symbolic gesture of radical feminism in the 70s? Bra burning.

And I can't leave the guys out here. Not only young women, but also young men need to be aware of the message their clothing sends to those around them. If a young man wears skin-tight pants and a "hand-me-up" t-shirt a younger sibling outgrew, his body may have a material covering plastered over it, but his form is clearly revealed.

When in doubt, try this little silhouette test. Stand sideways in front of a light and check out your shadow. Can you tell by your shadow if you are dressed or not? If it is questionable for even an instant, I would recommend changing.

And don't forget the PTL test! PTL stands for "praise the Lord." If you can lift your arms or bend over without exposing your midriff, other body parts or under garments, then you pass the PTL test! You won't have to worry as you worship, work or play! Be free!

One more thing while I'm on a roll ... I just have to wonder if the young men with the britches riding low and boxers hanging out are aware this look originated in prison. For safety reasons, inmates aren't allowed belts, and droopy drawers are the result. I guess "dress for success" isn't running through the minds of the young men modeling their wardrobes after prisoners. Are these convicts the role models our Christian young men should wish to emulate?

Dressing sensually (even our private undergarments) is taking a step *away* from purity and towards fulfilling provocative desires that steer us in the wrong direction. Modesty is a separation from worldliness and will, in fact, deter immorality in our lives.

Matthew Henry, a famous Bible scholar and author of the 1600s, wrote in his commentary, "Those that have broken the fences of modesty will never be held by the bonds of piety." Wow! If he could only see us now.

A young lady recently shared with me how upset she was when a guy she knew called her a prude. "Don't be upset!" I replied. "You should consider that a compliment!" She gave me that sideways look only a teenager can give, but she had to smile when I said, "Do you know what the word prude really means? It's a shortened form of prudent, which means wise. So he was actually giving you a compliment."

Throughout history, slaves have been the ones forced to go without proper clothing – even to the point of nakedness. Along with peasant girls and concubines, they wore short dresses indicating their sexual availability, while royalty and important people in cultures from Egypt to England wore floor-length flowing robes.

In Italy, female tourists must cover their shoulders and also their legs past their knees if they wish to visit inside many of the churches there. And though I am not Catholic, I like Pope Pius XII's opinion of what modest women should wear: "Below the knee, halfway down the arm, and two finger widths below the collarbone."

I'm not writing to press my personal dressing guidelines upon anyone, but I do hope you will give some thought and prayer to the issue. True modesty starts below the exterior. It's an issue of purity in thought and manner which manifests itself in the way we dress and conduct ourselves with humility and respect.

> *True modesty starts below the exterior. It's an issue of purity in thought and manner which manifests itself in the way we dress and conduct ourselves with humility and respect.*

Here are a couple of Scriptures to think about.

Behold, I come as a thief. Blessed is he that watcheth, and keepeth his garments, lest he walk naked, and they see his shame. (Revelation 16:15)

Pure religion and undefiled before God and the Father is this, To visit the fatherless and widows in their affliction, and to keep himself unspotted from the world. (James 1:27)

For further study, read Exodus 28:42-43 and Isaiah 47:2-3.

Jesus, you know my heart. You know I want to feel desirable and attractive – even cool, trendy and fashionable. Grow within me a desire to be attractive through my personality more than my appearance, especially avoiding exposing myself in ways that don't show respect to You or the body you gave me. Help me be honest with myself as I evaluate the motives behind the clothing I choose to wear.

Give me understanding that it's not just about me, it's about the world I live in, too. I want to be Your witness to my generation, but if I look and act just like the world, how will they see the difference in my life? How will they see You in me? Help me to be sensitive to the effect my wardrobe choices have on others, and help me to "watch my garments" and "keep myself unspotted from the world."

CHAPTER REVIEW AND APPLICATION

The major theme of this chapter is:

_____

_____

Explain the difference between the coverings Adam and Eve made and their adequacy vs. what God made for them.

_____

_____

How would you describe your "dressing language" and the way others perceive your character as a result?

_____

_____

Do you think the values and lifestyle choices of the group of people you are dressing like is reflective of your character and convictions?

_____

_____

How do our dressing choices affect others spiritually? Does that matter to you?

_____

_____

Explain in your own words how men are enticed to sin when young women dress immodestly.

_____

_____

What's the "no zone" and how should that impact our clothing choices?

_____

_____

Modesty is a separation from:

_____

Where does true modesty begin?

_____

_____

As you purpose to please God by honoring and respecting His Word in the area of modesty, take a moment to write your personal prayer to Him.

_____

_____

_____

_____

_____

_____

_____

_____

_____

_____

_____

In I Timothy chapters 4 and 5 the Bible speaks directly to young men and instructs them specifically in verse 5:2 to treat young women as sisters with absolute purity. *If we follow this guideline, we will be protected from falling to sexual sin.*

5

DON'T TOUCH!

The Fence of Purity

There are warning signs everywhere. They shout at us, "Don't walk on the grass!" "No parking!" "Don't touch, wet paint!" What's with all the "DON'Ts" and "NOs" anyway?

There are usually valid reasons for the warnings we see, but as we recall from our discussion of Robert Frost's poem, there is something in us that "doesn't love a wall" – we just don't like being told what we can or can't do. Oh, we agree that most people should follow the rules, but we could be the exception. The rules don't have to apply to *everyone*. Besides, *we* know what we are doing. We are in control. Just because other people aren't strong enough to handle temptation doesn't mean we aren't, right?

I was speaking to a young lady who was interested in a boy named Eric. She also happened to have a passion for potato chips.

We were driving down the road talking about this young man and how relationships can develop into more than we anticipate if we aren't careful. I said, "You know how you think you can open a bag of chips and eat just one? Well, it's like that with boys. You want to have just one kiss. You think you'll be happy with one, but that kiss is so sweet and exciting … you'll just have one more. The kisses keep coming, and before you know it, you've eaten the whole bag."

The young lady smiled, and I knew she had gotten the picture.

"You know what I'm going to call Eric from now on?" I said. "I'm going to call him Chip. Whenever I see you, I'm going to ask how Chip is doing."

She laughed, and over the next few weeks I did ask her about Chip, but it wasn't very long before she wasn't interested in him anymore.

I hope my young friend was glad she hadn't opened the "bag of chips" and she will remember this example the next time a tempting package comes along.

But wait! The Apostle Paul says to greet one another with a holy kiss, and he wrote most of the New Testament! That means it's okay to kiss, right?

Kissing a fellow believer – your brother or sister in the Lord – does not fall into the same category as romantic kissing. Paul was talking about the kind of kiss you'd give your mom, your dad, or your great aunt Louise.

In I Timothy chapters 4 and 5, the Bible speaks directly to young men and instructs them specifically in verse 5:2 to treat young women as sisters *with absolute purity*. If we follow this guideline, we will be protected from falling to sexual sin.

Let's talk "straight up" as my kids say. Romantic, premarital kissing is very intimate and is not an innocent act of greeting. No, premarital kissing, making out, whatever you want to call it, is rooted in emotion and sexual desire. It stirs up a passion that isn't lawful to be satisfied according to Scripture.

This type of behavior is not going to enhance your relationship. It will actually make it more difficult for you to get to know each other as you really are. Instead of using your time to discover your personalities, your goals, plans, dreams and convictions; it will draw your focus to the physical, cluttering your mind and distracting you from more important aspects of your relationship.

> *This type of behavior ...will draw your focus to the physical, cluttering your mind and distracting you from more important aspects of your relationship.*

Let's look at a term in the Bible called "defrauding." Defrauding means "to promise something one cannot or does not intend to deliver." We hear about fraud in the news when a con artist tricks a trusting senior citizen out of their life's savings with some investment scam – or someone pretends to be a medical doctor and people are injured by their negligence, etc. Of course these fraudulent acts are terrible and clearly sinful.

The Bible speaks against defrauding a brother (and this applies to sisters, too). The King James version words it like this:

That no man go beyond and defraud his brother in any matter: because that the Lord is the avenger of all such, as we also have forewarned you and testified. (I Thessalonians 4:6)

That might not be very clear on it's own in the King James English, so let's look at the verse in context in the NIV version:

It is God's will that you should be sanctified: that you should avoid sexual immorality; that each of you should learn to control his own body in a way that is holy and honorable, not in

47

passionate lust like the heathen, who do not know God; and that in this matter no one should wrong [defraud] *his brother or take advantage of him. The Lord will punish men for all such sins, as we have already told you and warned you. For God did not call us to be impure, but to live a holy life.*
(I Thessalonians 4:3-7)

Romantic kissing and other acts of sexual stimulation between single people blatantly arouse emotions and physical sensations without the freedom to follow through. You might not have considered that kissing someone is actually a form of fraud or cheating, but it is, because you are not intending to "deliver." And if you are, well, we should just skip this section and jump ahead a couple of chapters!

Not only are these activities fraudulent and cheating in their very nature, but if you engage in them, you could be stealing, too. If you don't marry your current flame, you will have taken what belongs to their spouse. That is theft! What a concept!

So we need to be cautious with something as simple as kissing, and also follow the other "don't touch" signs posted along the path of our relationships. Let's keep our hands and lips and everything else to ourselves! And remember, these caution signs were not installed by the police department who follow us around on the road of life writing up tickets to generate fines and meet quotas. Our loving Father has given us instructions that will keep us safely on the narrow path of His blessing – leading us exactly where we want to go.

Jesus, help me keep every part of myself holy and set apart for Your good pleasure. You designed me with a natural curiosity and desire to share in the pleasure and intimacy of kissing and touching. Help me treasure the gift of romantic love so deeply that I will reserve every aspect of my sexuality until You have blessed and sanctified both the time and the person You decide is best for me in the lifelong relationship of marriage. Help single people everywhere treat one another with "absolute purity" as you outlined in Your holy Word.

CHAPTER REVIEW AND APPLICATION

The major theme of this chapter is:

_____

_____

How does a godly kiss of greeting differ from romantic kissing in its purpose and results?

_____

_____

_____

According to I Timothy 5:2, how did the Apostle Paul instruct godly young men to treat young ladies?

_____

How would you define absolute purity?

_____

_____

What does it mean to defraud?

_____

_____

Explain how the concept of defrauding applies to romantic kissing and touching.

_____

_____

_____

How could getting physically involved deter the development of a relationship between a young man and a young woman?

_____

_____

_____

As you purpose to please God by honoring and respecting His Word in the area of purity, take a moment to write your personal prayer to Him.

_____

_____

_____

_____

_____

_____

_____

_____

_____

_____

_____

When we wait for God's best, we avoid getting caught in the potential dangers of the dating trap. Compromising our future for today's short-term pleasure is not a good trade.

6

GIVE IT A REST!

The Gateway of Early Dating

Have you heard the saying, "Let sleeping dogs lie?" It's good advice for those who don't want to become human doggy biscuits. The Bible tells us it's wise to leave other things at rest, as well. Three times the Song of Solomon admonishes "do not arouse or awaken love" before it's time. (Song of Solomon 2:7, 3:5, and 8:4)

As we discussed in the previous chapter, arousing sexual desire before having the freedom to fulfill that desire only leads to frustration – and possibly a hard fall. Those involved set their feet on a slippery slope and wonder why they nose-dive into sexual sin.

Another important reason for unmarried people to leave their passion at rest is to protect themselves from becoming desensitized. Each time a person gives in to self-indulgent behavior, it becomes easier to ignore the inner voice of conscience and its warning signals. The nervousness disappears as the conscience is numbed, and people find themselves plunging to deeper and deeper levels of involvement.

In the beginning, the mere brushing of fingertips can send tingles down your spine, but after you become comfortable with this phase of physical touch, the excitement settles down. That's when the search begins for new ways of achieving that euphoric feeling. Therein lies the problem as "Pandora's Box" is opened and the temptation to progress further in a physical relationship grows stronger and more demanding.

And if you will allow me to be very plain with you, we can apply this principle to self-gratification as well. It may seem a harmless thing to do, but we can choose to "awaken" ourselves and jump into the sexual arena with or without a partner. We can indulge ourselves in physical pleasure and stimulate the growth of our sexuality, or we can purpose to resist fueling the fires of passion before they burn out of control. Remember, what you feed will grow.

Do you know how to boil a live frog? Just imagine, if we placed a frog in a pan of boiling water, would he sit in that pan and allow himself to boil to death? No! He would use his little flippers and jump right out.

However, if you were to put that same frog in a pot of nice, room temperature water, he might like that and stay in – even enjoy a refreshing swim. Little by little, we could raise the temperature until it reached the boiling point. The result would be a dead frog, one boiled alive in a pot he could have easily escaped.

How could this happen? Why wouldn't the frog jump out of the pot? Desensitization. The frog wouldn't notice the slight elevations in temperature until it was too late to jump out and he was on somebody's appetizer plate next to a cup of tangy dipping sauce.

Statistics show a correlation between early dating and early sexual activity (see table below). There is a direct connection between "waking up" in your dating life and early sexual involvement.

The Younger the Dating, The Sooner The Sexual Activity

From the *Journal of Adolescent Research* 1986; 1(3): 361-371

Authors: Brent C. Miller, J. Kelly McCoy and Terrance D. Olson

Age dating began	Percentage of girls reporting intercourse by graduation	Percentage of boys reporting intercourse by graduation
12	90%	71%
13	53%	100%
14	49%	72%
15	37%	48%
16	18%	16%
17	13%	21%

- Early dating, especially early steady dating, was related to permissive attitudes and to premarital sexual experience among both male and female.

- Of ninth graders in steady dating relationships, 70% of boys and 60% of girls say they've had sex.

In his book *I Kissed Dating Goodbye*, author Joshua Harris discussed the differences between what he identified as "smart love" and "dumb love." He described smart love as "sincere, God-focused love that is concerned for others," and dumb love as "selfish and flirtatious." Harris also made the point that dating practices in our Western culture are little more than "a training ground for divorce." If one person doesn't work out, we can dump them and move on to someone else. What a concept.

> *When we wait for God's direction instead of jumping from relationship to relationship, we show our appreciation for His Word and the godly values of sincere love, respect and commitment.*

When we wait for God's direction instead of jumping from relationship to relationship, we show our appreciation for His Word and the godly values of sincere love, respect and commitment.

And don't forget that when you are ready to consider a lifetime commitment, "dating for Jesus" isn't the way to go. We don't "flirt to convert" or even consider a romantic relationship with non-Christians.

Don't team up with those who are unbelievers. How can righteousness be a partner with wickedness? How can light live with darkness? (II Corinthians 6:14 NLT)

So should we date ... or wait?

When we wait for God's best, we avoid getting caught in the potential dangers of the dating trap. Compromising our future for today's short-term pleasure is not a good trade. There's a better way to live. Besides, falling in and out of "love" and getting hurt really isn't fun.

And it's all right to feel you're missing out on some things! You are! A true Christian's walk is marked by self-sacrifice.

And so, dear brothers and sisters, I plead with you to give your bodies to God. Let them be a living and holy sacrifice — the kind He will accept. When you think of what He has done for you, is this too much to ask? Don't copy the behavior and customs of this world, but let God transform you into a new person by changing the way you think. Then you will know what God wants you to do, and you will know how good and pleasing and perfect His will really is. (Romans 12:1-2 NLT)

Paul said we are to be *living* sacrifices. The problem with living sacrifices is that they want to crawl off the altar when the fire gets hot!

But let's focus on the positive here. You may be "missing out" on what seems to be a good time, but you are also missing out on a lot of heartache, pain and regrets. And you get the added bonus of having a clear conscience. You won't have a head full of memories of some other person running through your mind during your married life. Our memories don't have delete keys, as convenient as that would be.

With all this in mind, don't be disappointed if you don't have a boyfriend or girlfriend. Know that it's okay to be different than your friends, within the church and without. No matter how others choose to live their lives, as Christians, we should be viewing any potential romantic relationships through God's perspective.

Dating is <u>not</u> a recreational activity. Putt-putt golf is a recreational activity. It is <u>not</u> a game to play with people's emotions – including your own.

Lord, it's so tempting to jump into a relationship because it's what I want to do – because I think someone's cute, nice or fun – because I want to feel attractive and desirable. Help me to wait for Your best for my life. I know that by following in the paths of godly wisdom I will avoid many pitfalls and problems.

Thank You for Your Word, Jesus, and give me the strength to live by my convictions regardless of any loneliness or pressure I may feel. I know I can do all things through You – and that includes being patient and accepting of Your timing and plans. And as I wait, put a passion in my heart to work for You, building Your kingdom and serving others.

CHAPTER REVIEW AND APPLICATION

The major theme of this chapter is:

_____

_____

How do you boil a live frog?

_____

_____

What is desensitization? How can it impact your conscience, and possibly your choices?

_____

_____

What do statistics tell us about the correlation between early dating and the likelihood of premarital sexual involvement?

_____

_____

What problems do you think you might experience by marrying a nonbeliever instead of a believer?

_____

_____

What blessings do you think you would experience by marrying a believer instead of a nonbeliever?

_____

_____

_____

Define "dumb" love?

_____

Define "smart" love?

_____

Explain how the Western style of dating could be considered a "training ground" for divorce.

_____

_____

As you purpose to please God by honoring and respecting His Word in the area of dating, take a moment to write your personal prayer to Him.

_____

_____

_____

_____

_____

_____

_____

_____

_____

_____

_____

_____

If we barrel through the fence of sexual purity as a single person, can we expect it to remain solidly intact once we are married?

7

WHY WAIT?

The Fence of Marital Fidelity
(Before and After the Wedding)

No one wants more for their children than their parents. I am so looking forward to my daughters' bridal showers and all the shopping, planning and excitement of preparing for their weddings. I want to stand at the front of the church as the wedding music begins to play and see my girls walk down the center aisle on their Daddy's arm wearing a beautiful white gown with a flowing train and flower petals strewn all around. I want all of their dreams to come true and to share in the joy of it all. I want the same for my son, as well (without the white dress).

Unfortunately, friends and dates don't always have the same long-sighted goals as parents. Your peers might not be thinking about the long-term effects of your short-term decisions. The philosophies of youth often proclaim live for the moment ... seize the day ... go for the gusto! Why wait until after marriage to enjoy the pleasures of sex when you could be having fun right now?

I encourage you to listen to the Word of God and the voices of those who love you the most. Words don't mean much, and you need to think hard about it. Who sticks by you through all your ups and downs? Who has more invested in you? Who cares more for your future? Who has your best, long-term interests at heart – your running buddies, or the ones who gave you life?

If we barrel through the fence of sexual purity as a single person, can we expect it to remain solidly intact once we are married? Here's a crucial question ... If the person you are with now is willing to compromise the principles of God's Word in the area of sexuality before marriage, how can you be confident they will remain faithful to their promise of fidelity to you in the future?

If the person you are with now is willing to compromise the principles of God's Word in the area of sexuality before marriage, how can you be confident they will remain faithful to their promise of fidelity to you in the future?

Another concept I've attempted to transmit to my girls is that by keeping themselves pure as a single person, they are being faithful to their future husbands *right now*. Imagine a young couple becomes intimately involved. Their future spouses could be living in another state. They may have never met, but they are cheating on them with the person they are currently being sexually active with.

If you were married, would you kiss someone other than your spouse? If you were married, would you want your spouse fondling someone else ... or worse?

It really is worth the wait. King Solomon had a lot to say on the subject. He married a beautiful virgin he described as an "enclosed garden." That's a great word picture for the enclosure of virginity. The word "paradise" is actually derived from an ancient Persian word that means enclosed garden.

Solomon described his bride as a paradise, a private place sealed off from all others. It was a place filled with wonderful fragrances and luscious fruits reserved just for him. It was full of life, containing fountains of flowing waters. This garden was a sacred place where his bride shared an intimacy him no one else could know. She was exclusively his. Isn't that romantic?

A garden enclosed is my sister, my spouse; a spring shut up, a fountain sealed. Thy plants are an orchard of pomegranates, with pleasant fruits; camphire, with spikenard, Spikenard and saffron; calamus and cinnamon, with all trees of frankincense;

myrrh and aloes, with all the chief spices: A fountain of gardens,
a well of living waters, and streams from Lebanon. (Song of
Solomon 4:12-15)

Scholars believe the following verse is Solomon's response after he
came together with his new bride for the first time.

I am come into my garden, my sister, my spouse: I have gathered
my myrrh with my spice; I have eaten my honeycomb with my
honey; I have drunk my wine with my milk: eat, O friends; drink,
yea, drink abundantly, O beloved. (Song of Solomon 5:1)

It sounds like Solomon has been to the mountain top and enjoyed the
view! He is recommending to his friends that they share in the same
type of relationship he has experienced in the private paradise of his
virgin bride. Considering Solomon was the wisest man who ever lived,
we would do well to heed his advice!

If the gate to your garden is unlocked, the beauty inside is vulnerable
and subject to being trampled on. Some people have revolving doors on
their gardens, and nothing is growing inside but weeds. Why is it that
those involved in all the "pleasure" seem to be the ones searching most
desperately for true happiness through sad, vacant eyes? When someone
opens themselves to sexual relationships, shouldn't they be more
fulfilled? The answer is no. It's another deceptive trick of satan. They
have given away a sacred treasure for stolen pleasure leaving themselves
feeling empty, used, and cheap. You ARE worth waiting for!

Lord, I see that the fence of virginity is a key test of my trust in You. Help me, Jesus, to keep my gate locked and my enclosed garden private until You give me the key to open it at the public exchange of my marriage vows. Help me keep from "jumping the fence" before it's time so that my marriage will begin on a solid foundation without regret and the doubt of future fidelity that results from premarital sexual activity. My trust is in You, and I want to wait for all the right reasons ... first, to please You; but secondly, because marital intimacy is a beautiful plan based on respect, honor and integrity. Help me to internalize these concepts and put them into practice in my relationships.

CHAPTER REVIEW AND APPLICATION

The major theme of this chapter is:

_____

_____

As a single Christian, are you looking forward to having a church wedding? If so, how could losing your virginity beforehand affect your hopes and dreams for the future?

_____

_____

_____

Compare how being unfaithful to God's principles of sexual purity in your single life could carry over into your married life.

_____

_____

_____

As a single person, how are you being faithful to your future mate in the here and now?

_____

_____

How did King Solomon describe his virgin bride?

_____

_____

Did he seem pleased with her, even though she was inexperienced in the ways to satisfy him sexually?

_____

What word in our modern language is derived from the ancient Persian word for "enclosed garden?"

_____

Why do you think those involved in all the "pleasure" of sex seem to be the ones searching for happiness the most?

_____

_____

Have you made a commitment to keep your garden a sacred place for your spouse?

_____

If you haven't yet, would you like to do that now?

_____

If so, take a moment to read the following, then insert your name, sign and date it on the line provided:

I, _____, want to make a firm, written commitment to myself and to God to remain sexually pure until my wedding night. I want to experience all the joys that God has prepared for me in the beautiful intimate relationship shared between a man and his wife. Please help me, Jesus, to remember this promise and to make wise decisions to be true to it, to my future spouse, and always to You.

_____

Signature   Date

As you purpose to please God by honoring and respecting His Word in the area of marital fidelity, take a moment to write your personal prayer to Him.

_____

_____

_____

_____

_____

_____

_____

_____

_____

_____

_____

Sexual sin is like no other sin. It can hurt you in every way: physically, emotionally, mentally, and spiritually.

8

TRUTH OR CONSEQUENCES

The Gateway of Sexual Promiscuity
And its Potential Repercussions

Please note: this chapter contains plain language about sexually transmitted diseases.

Truth or Consequences was a radio program originating in the 1940s. It later became a TV show that ran until the late 1980s. To play the game participants answered trivia questions before "Beulah the Buzzer" was sounded. If they failed the "Truth" portion of the show, they would have to face some wacky consequences — usually a crazy or embarrassing stunt.

"Truth or consequences" is a phrase easily applied to our Christian walk. When we desire to live a pure life set apart for the Lord, we must

74

live the Truth, or we will face consequences. And these consequences are much more severe than embarrassing practical jokes or monkeyshines. Of course, this is a play on words, but Truth or consequences is a reality in our day-to-day lives.

The Scripture tells us in Proverbs 4:18-19 that the path of the godly and the path of the ungodly are very different (actually walking in different directions). When we walk on the path of Truth, it's like walking into the sunrise that gets brighter every day. When I think about that I can almost feel the sun warming my face on a beautiful day. But the way of the wicked is like darkness. They can't even see what's tripping them up. I don't want to be lost in the dark, not able to see the potholes and pitfalls ahead of me. That's scary.

And what's sad is that the devil has once again twisted God's beautiful plans, just like in the Garden of Eden. He polluted something precious degenerating it into something cheap, filthy and even dangerous. God designed sexual intimacy. It's a beautiful expression of love that creates life. We're not going to cover the risk of an unplanned pregnancy here, but we will look at how sexual intimacy before marriage can lead to death — spiritually and sometimes even physically.

Do you not know that the wicked will not inherit the kingdom of God? Do not be deceived: Neither the sexually immoral nor idolaters nor adulterers nor male prostitutes nor homosexual offenders nor thieves nor the greedy nor drunkards nor slanderers nor swindlers will inherit the kingdom of God.
(I Corinthians 6:9-10 NIV)

Colossians 3:5 instructs us to "kill off" everything in our lives that is connected with the way of death, including sexual promiscuity. We're talking about missing out on eternal life with Jesus for a quick physical thrill. That, my friend, is a terrible consequence.

Of course, we always have the repentance option in our back pocket, right? God is merciful. We can ask Him to forgive us later, right? I guess we've all had those thoughts at one time or another, and God is merciful. However, we shouldn't live with the presumption that we can play games with God. We could get caught in the tentacles of a trap we can't free ourselves from. The web of sin is sticky.

✍

Beyond our spiritual being, we must also consider our physical being. A lot of Christians opt out of taking sex ed classes in public schools (which is probably a good choice considering some of the curricula being used). Many young people are home-schooled or attend private schools where they often don't learn about the very real possibility of contracting sexually transmitted diseases (STDs).

The truth is many diseases can be contracted through sexual intimacy. They have varying levels of difficulty in spreading, but the only sure way to avoid them is to abstain from sexual activity. And I'm not just talking about intercourse. These can be contracted in your mouth and other areas of your body. The "protection" you buy from the drugstore will not guarantee you won't contract these diseases. As a matter of fact, these drugstore methods have been shown <u>ineffective</u> in deterring the spread of some diseases altogether, and the end result of a romantic interest could prove to be a "fatal attraction."

ℒ

Please keep in mind that the following statistics are annual. *Every year these numbers replicate themselves, and this is in America alone.* This information was compiled by John R. Diggs, Jr., MD, and Nancy Couch, MD, in March 2005. Their complete overview of STDs is available at www.parentspromotinginnocence.org.

- Every year there are an estimated 700,000 new cases of gonorrhea. Gonorrhea is caused by bacteria and spreads very easily affecting not only sexual organs, but also potentially the liver, throat, skin, joints, blood and brain.

- Annually there are 32,000 new cases of syphilis, which can result in brain, spinal cord and heart injury — even death.

- Each year there are an astounding 1 million new cases of herpes. This is a painful, incurable, permanent infection which can be life-threatening.

- Acquired Immune Deficiency Syndrome (AIDS) is a virus that attacks 40,000 new people each year. AIDS is incurable and permanent. It weakens the immune system, which results in life-threatening pneumonias, intestinal infections, neurological disorders, cancer and death.

- Hepatitis B is a potentially fatal virus. Many recover after suffering jaundice, nausea and vomiting, but some retain chronic illnesses and suffer liver failure.

- Over 5.5 million cases of Human Papiloma Virus (HPV) occur each year. Many don't suffer from warts, but others do and must endure treatments of caustic chemicals, lasers and creams — sometimes drastic hysterectomy and colon removal. This virus is the easiest to contract of all known STDs and runs rampant on university campuses. It also has the potential to cause cancer.

These are just some of the STDs out there. We must be aware of these hidden epidemics and recognize the risks. It's easy to think that we will be safe because the person we're with isn't promiscuous. But we really don't know everything about each other, and there is a pyramid effect we must consider. With just one indiscretion you could be sharing "cooties" from hundreds of other people.

Say your partner was only with one other person one time ... he/she didn't even go "all the way," but was still exposed to every one that person was with ... and every one that person was with ... and every one that person was with. Just imagine, as you cozy up to your sweetheart, the saliva and bodily fluids of a hundred other people are right there just waiting to mingle with yours. It's not pretty.

> *Flee from sexual immorality. All other sins a man commits are outside his body, but he who sins sexually sins against his own body.* (I Corinthians 6:18)

Hebrews 13:4 says we should honor marriage and guard the sacredness of sexual intimacy between a husband and wife. Sexual sin is like no other sin. It can hurt you in every way; physically, emotionally, mentally, and spiritually. God's Word is very clear here.

Lord, I thank You for the protection You provide for me when I live according to Your Word. I don't want my physical desires to open a gate I may never be able to close again. Help me remember that although all sin has consequences, sexual sin is in a category all its own. Give me the strength of character and determination of conviction to keep myself safe inside the parameters of purity in my relationships. You really do know what's best, and I trust in Your plan for my life, Jesus.

CHAPTER REVIEW AND APPLICATION

The major theme of this chapter is:

_____

_____

According to Psalms, how does the path of the ungodly differ from the path of the just?

_____

_____

Will fornicators or adulterers be admitted to heaven?

_____

What does Colossians 3:5 say we should do to anything in our lives connected to the way of death?

_____

Although God forgives us, are there often life-changing consequences associated with sexual sin?

_____

What could some of these consequences be?

_____

_____

What does STD stand for?

_____

Can STDs be fatal?

_____

Can you get an STD even if you don't "go all they way?"

_____

Besides abstaining from sexual activities, is there any sure way to avoid contracting STDs?

_____

Explain how sexual sin is like no other sin in the way it affects our lives.

_____

_____

As you consider the serious consequences of sexual sin, take a moment to write your personal prayer to God on this subject.

_____

_____

_____

_____

_____

_____

_____

_____

_____

_____

_____

... *God always has an escape route away from temptation. Look for the way out ... and take it!*

DON'T GIVE PLACE TO THE DEVIL

The Gateway of Entertaining Temptation

"Don't give place to the devil." We've heard that verse before, but let's look at it a little more in-depth.

Be ye angry, and sin not: let not the sun go down upon your wrath: Neither give place to the devil. (Ephesians 4:26-27)

The word for "place" in the Greek is "topos" which actually means "ground." It's the root for the word topography – you know, soil, where you put your feet down and where things grow. So, let's apply that. We can't give the enemy any ground (any place to stand or let ungodly things grow) in our lives ... and that includes our thought lives, also.

How do we make that happen? One way is by refusing to entertain temptation. If we dwell on the things that are tempting us, we will be much more susceptible to actually participate in ungodly behavior.

But each one is tempted when, by his own evil desire, he is dragged away and enticed. Then, after desire has conceived, it gives birth to sin; and sin, when it is full-grown, gives birth to death. (James 1:14-15 NIV)

Don't let your temptations connect with your actions conceiving and giving birth to sin. There was a sign in a college dormitory that read, "Lead me not into temptation, I can find it myself." That's the truth, but Scripture gives us good advice in I Corinthians 10:13. It says God always has an escape route away from temptation. Look for the way out, and take it!

Flee the evil desires of youth, and pursue righteousness, faith, love and peace, along with those who call on the Lord out of a pure heart. (II Timothy 2:22)

Flee means to run away, so think about this. If you're running away from something, then you must be running towards something else. When we flee from sin, we run in God's direction. Do you remember being little and running to someone that would pick you up and twirl you around? I see God that way. He's waiting to grab you and give you a good twirl … with a big "attaboy" pat on the back.

Let's look a little further into "not giving place." I would go so far as to say that you and I cannot give *ourselves* place to fall into the devil's hands. Satan is looking for ways to take advantage of us, so we must be aware of his sneaky methods by remaining spiritually alert. One careless moment is the devil's opportunity to wreak havoc in our lives (see I Peter 5:8-9).

The following are some safeguards we can apply to keep the gate of temptation closed.

1. Hang out in coed groups in safe places. The "place" we can't give to the devil is any place we would be tempted to give in to sin … in the car, the bedroom, at home alone, etc. You might think your commitments will keep you, but just avoid the opportunity altogether. **If we keep ourselves from being alone with a person of the opposite sex in compromising situations, we will always be safe from falling to sexual temptation.**

   If you and your date are alone, not only will the temptation be harder, but you are most assuredly being watched by someone. Even if you are completely innocent in what you are doing, you may be destroying your Christian witness. Your reputation, and even how people view God and Christianity in general, can be marred in your community by the mere appearance of wrongdoing. If we call ourselves Christians, our actions should be God-pleasing more than pleasure-seeking, and our conduct must not give others "place" to doubt our walk with God or the validity of His Word.

2. We need to use wisdom about spending time in "places" others will be participating in ungodly activities. I'm sure we all hope for opportunities to witness to unsaved friends, but we don't want to attend parties where we know we will be exposed to substance abuse, immoral music, sensual dancing etc. Are we really being honest with ourselves thinking we could have a positive Christian impact in such an environment?

I recently heard Chuck Swindoll on the radio. He was saying that after a big rain, if you go outside with a white glove on and smear it all over the yard, the yard never gets "glovey." Oh, no. The glove always gets muddy, but the yard never gets "glovey." So keep out of muddy situations. God will give you the right opportunity to speak into the lives of your friends … and it would be best if they were sober anyway, right?

3. Another "place" you don't want to give the devil is in your thoughts. Don't play with sin even in your mind. Our thought lives can be the devil's playground even though we haven't actually become physically involved

in sin. "For as he thinketh in his heart, so is he ..." (Proverbs 23:7).

And when we mess up (and we ALL do), we need to immediately get it right with God by asking His forgiveness. This will keep the enemy from gaining even one little toehold of guilt in our lives. If we allow sin to steep in our hearts, satan plays a mountain climber using his pick and rope to climb and conquer the peaks in our spiritual lives.

We all have areas of weakness, but God has given us a beautiful word picture of how He gives each of us victory in our struggles.

The Lord God is my strength, and He will make my feet like hind's feet, and He will make me to walk upon mine high places. (Habakkuk 3:19)

God compares us to mountain goats leaping gracefully from high place to high place upon the mountains with strength and agility ... but not just any high places ... our own individual high places. God knows our unique personal weaknesses, and He wants to give us the strength to live above them, not beneath their influence.

If you are continually tempted by something in your life, get rid of it. God says to pluck out your eye if it's offending you (Matthew 5:29). That may seem severe, but God uses this drastic illustration to relay a crucial message. We must sever, at whatever cost, anything that will drag our souls to eternal hell. Nothing's worth it. Ditch the music. Pitch the video games. Break the DVDs. Burn the books. Skip the parties. Avoid immoral friendships. Change your thought patterns.

I'm not saying it's easy, but it's worth it. If a person was praying that God would help them stop drinking, why would they keep a pint of liquor in their closet? Or hang out with people that are drinkers? Get rid of the hindrances and temptations. It will help you live in freedom. **Make a commitment now that will keep you secure in the temptations to come.** Daniel's commitment to God as a teenager kept him safe the rest of his life — even in a den of hungry lions.

Lord, your Word says that we should watch and pray we would not enter into temptation. I'm asking for Your help to make wise choices in the activities and situations I get myself involved in. I don't want to give the devil any place to get a foothold in my life. Help me, Jesus, in my personal struggles to leap over the temptations rather than be buried under them and the weight of the resulting condemnation. When I'm in a compromising situation, show me the escape route and give me the courage to take it. And when I fail, let me have the sensitivity to turn to You without delay for forgiveness and restoration.

CHAPTER REVIEW AND APPLICATION

The major theme of this chapter is:

_____

_____

What does the Greek word for "place" mean in Ephesians 4:27, and how can we apply that to our lives spiritually?

_____

_____

_____

One important safeguard to keep from falling into sin is to refuse to entertain:

_____

How can hanging out in coed groups instead of coupling off be a safeguard to your purity?

_____

_____

How would avoiding places where you know sinful activities are occurring be a safeguard to you?

_____

_____

How would keeping your mind from dwelling on temptations benefit your morality?

_____

_____

Everyone sins. As we mature in Christ, hopefully that will occur with less and less frequency; however, when we fall, what is the best thing we can do and when?

_____

_____

If you are continually being tempted by something, what strategies could you use to overcome that temptation?

_____

_____

_____

As you purpose to please God by honoring and respecting His Word, take a moment to write your personal prayer to Him asking for His help in refusing to entertain temptation.

_____

_____

_____

_____

_____

_____

_____

_____

_____

_____

_____

_____

... Adam was in a committed relationship with God before Eve came on the scene. The pursuit of a spouse cannot take a higher priority in our lives than our relationship with God.

10

ARE YOU IN A COMMITTED RELATIONSHIP?

The Fence of Godly Priorities

Sometimes it's tempting to "relax" commitments to purity when people are in serious relationships. After all, if two people intend to spend the rest of their lives together, what difference does it make if they begin their intimate physical relationship before the official wedding ceremony? A marriage certificate is just a piece of paper. Besides, who will ever know?

Many people have used this line of thinking to rationalize their sin, but there are serious flaws in this reasoning. First, and of utmost importance, is the motive. Should we base our actions on what we think we can get away with, or seek God's blessings and favor in our lives – especially in the <u>lifetime</u> commitment of marriage?

Rationalizing perceived loopholes is more than wrong, it's presumptuous. No one knows what the future really holds. You and your intended may never make it to the altar, no matter how devoted you are to each other. Accidents happen. Sickness comes. People break up. A huge percentage of engagements fail. How would you feel if you were having sex with a person you had every intention of marrying, and they broke up with you before the wedding?

But let's consider the best case scenario. Everything worked out great, just like you hoped and planned. You got married, and life's wonderful. But just one thing ... you and your spouse know that you began your marriage outside of God's will. I'm not talking about guilt, because God generously forgives us when we truly seek Him in repentance, but you've missed out on a blessing that could have been a real strength to your marriage. Our loving Father pours out blessings upon those who are obedient to His Word.

The Lord shall greatly bless thee, if thou only carefully hearken unto the voice of the Lord thy God. (Deuteronomy 15:4-5)

Think of how special your wedding night will be when you follow God's perfect plan. You and your fiance are crazy in love. You've kept yourselves pure and stand in bridal white honorably before God, your families, friends and church. You exchange wedding vows and receive blessings from everyone gathered with you on your special day.

After the reception, you enter the honeymoon suite nervous and inexperienced, but excited and confident that God is smiling down on you and the sure foundation on which you have begun your marriage.

Now you are free to enjoy the gift that God has given you without guilt or shame. You and your spouse experience the beauty of intimacy in a pure and delightful way.

Marriage should be honored by all, and the marriage bed kept pure, for God will judge the adulterer and all the sexually immoral. (Hebrews 13:4 NIV)

$$\mathscr{O}$$

We all look for that "special someone" to fulfill our dreams and make us happy. Do you know where that desire came from? God Himself! It's a good thing! God designed woman for man and the entire spectrum of the relationships they would share: emotional, spiritual and physical. God's plan was to bring a completeness to Adam that he hadn't experienced when he was alone (Genesis 2:18).

> *The pursuit of a spouse cannot take a higher priority than our relationship with God. Our commitment to our Creator is more important than our relationship with any of the people He created ...*

Have you considered that *Adam was in a committed relationship with God before Eve came on the scene?* The pursuit of a spouse cannot take a higher priority in our lives than our relationship with God. Our commitment to our Creator is more important than our relationship with any of the people He created … no matter how they make our little hearts pitter-patter!

I hope you signified your commitment to purity in written form at the end of Chapter 7. It will strengthen your resolve to see it in writing. Feel free to use your own words and write it on a separate paper to tuck in your Bible and review from time to time. Then when you do get in a serious relationship, you can share this to make sure you and your boyfriend or girlfriend are on the same page and have similar expectations for your future. You may want to make a written pact together declaring your united pledge to purity in your relationship.

To really seal the deal, you could make yourself accountable to your parents or a trusted youth worker, singles minister, pastor, etc. When you open yourself to those in authority over you and allow yourself to be accountable to them in the area of purity, you will erect a sturdy fence of protection around yourself and the one you love.

Lord, whenever the time comes for You to bring me into a relationship with my future spouse, I pray that my relationship with You will still maintain the highest priority in my life. You are more important than anything else, especially a few stolen minutes of pleasure outside of Your will. Help me, Jesus, to be committed to Your Word and faithful to You and my fiance' throughout the time before our wedding. I want to begin my marriage with Your unreserved blessing and favor.

CHAPTER REVIEW AND APPLICATION

The major theme of this chapter is:

_____

_____

What are some of the flaws in thinking that it's okay to begin an intimate relationship before marriage?

_____

_____

Who created the gift of sexual intimacy? And how does that impact your thinking of it?

_____

_____

According to Deuteronomy 15:4-5, how does God respond to those who carefully listen to His Word?

_____

_____

Do you think the eternal blessings and rewards of God are enough to keep you pure in your single life? Should they be?

_____

How could you keeping things in perspective to help you in your day-to-day decisions?

_____

_____

Considering the physical, emotional and spiritual aspects involved, how do you think your wedding night and marriage would benefit if you waited until that time to become physically intimate with your spouse?

_____

_____

Why do you think God created Adam and established His relationship and calling with him before He gave Eve to him as his wife? How could you apply this to your life?

_____

_____

_____

As you purpose to please God by putting your relationship with Him before all others, take a moment to write your personal prayer asking for His help with your priorities and reaffirming your commitment to Him.

_____

_____

_____

_____

_____

_____

_____

_____

_____

_____

_____

Guard the gate of your hearing internally by refusing to dwell on thoughts contrary to God's Word ... and also externally by controlling your environment and the entertainment choices you make.

11

OH BE CAREFUL, LITTLE EARS

The Gateway of Hearing

Spoken words enter directly into our hearts through the gateway of hearing. Many Scriptures address the connection between hearing and our walk with God.

*"Faith cometh by **hearing**, and **hearing** by the word of God."* (Romans 10:17)

*"**Hear**, ye children, the instruction of a father, and attend to know understanding."* (Proverbs 4:1)

*"**Hear** thou, my son, and be wise, and guide thine heart in the way."* (Proverbs 23:19)

*It is better to **hear** the rebuke of the wise, than for a man to **hear** the song of fools.* (Ecclesiastes 7:4-6)

*While it is said, To day if ye will **hear** his voice, harden not your hearts...* (Hebrews 3:15)

God is always speaking to us. He wants to give us guidance and direction, but there are many other "voices" vying for our attention as well. We learn to recognize God's voice through reading His Word and spending time in His presence.

My sheep listen to my voice, I know them, and they follow me. (John 10:27)

We are receptors, constantly picking up signals and messages that are being transmitted all around us. It's like we're radios, and there are messages coming at us on different wavelengths from all around. We need to be aware of the stations we "tune in" to and evaluate the sources of the messages we are receiving.

It's like we're radios, and there are messages coming at us on different wavelengths from all around. We need to be aware of the stations we "tune in" to and evaluate the sources of the messages we are receiving.

Of course, we live in the world, but because we are Christians, we are not "of" the world. Look at a submarine, for example. A submarine is designed to travel under the water's surface; however, the external environment cannot be allowed inside the ship. If that happened, the ship would sink, and the sailors on board would perish. Any possible safety breaches would never be ignored. Alarms would sound, and the immediate repair of the ship would take priority over everything.

As believers, we are now citizens of heaven. This world is not our home any longer. Like the sailors on the submarine, we travel through a foreign environment that must not be allowed to penetrate into our beings (body, mind and spirit), or we may find ourselves drowning in a sea of worldliness.

It's impossible to control our surroundings 100 percent of the time. As we go about our daily lives we will hear profanity, crude humor and angry, rebellious words. However, purposefully choosing to limit our exposure to the places where we know these negative conversations are more likely to occur will help keep the "water" out of our "submarines."

Let's turn our focus away from the negative things we should be avoiding and on to the positive things we are free to enjoy. There are many wonderful opportunities and means available to feed our souls with good things (see Philippians 4:8). Awesome Christian music is available in any style you care to listen to. There are music and teaching CDs and DVDs available to purchase. Christian radio and television programming is at hand 24/7. Christian fiction and nonfiction writings are free for the taking in public libraries. Christian comedians and theatrical groups are ready to entertain us. And we hopefully have godly friends to talk to who encourage us in our walks with the Lord.

I'm not advocating that everything we listen to or participate in MUST be God-centered. There are some neutral things as well. I like classical music, and much of it is not religious in nature. We sometimes take the kids bowling on a Saturday afternoon (when the bowling alley is smoke free and quiet). But I don't want to go on a Saturday night when people are drinking, smoking, swearing and all kinds of vulgar music is playing. It comes down to making good choices to keep our environment as clean as possible while still enjoying the life God has given us.

Of course, we can't have a chapter on hearing without discussing "rock and roll" music. Did you know that the term itself is a street name for fornication? Rock music's promotion of immorality, drug abuse, and perversion -- even suicide and satanism -- has wrecked the lives of many. I strongly advise you avoid rock music as much as possible, along with hip-hop and rap, which send the same messages in different musical styles. However, please be mindful that it's not just the *style* of music to consider, it is definitely the *message* behind it that is the most important concern.

Did you know that satan was created as a beautiful musical angel?

...every precious stone was thy covering...the workmanship of thy tabrets and of thy pipes was prepared in thee in the day that thou wast created. (Ezekiel 28:13)

Music was built into satan's very being, and he is willing and able to use his gift to deceive and trap God's people. It's his specialty – his area of expertise. So be careful, okay? Remember, GIGO – garbage in: garbage out!

$$\mathscr{D}$$

Here's something else to think about. It's more than just the words we hear that affect us: the words we speak have a huge impact, too. When we speak, we use two methods of communication at once (hearing and speaking), sending even stronger messages to our hearts through our spoken words. That's why it's really effective to read the Bible out loud in your personal study time. You use your eyes, ears and mouth all together. It can add a new dimension to your devotions.

The words we hear aren't always audible. Sometimes we hear them through inner voices. Consider this: satan has the ability to speak to us in first person using our own voices. He attempts to deceive us into thinking his planted "thoughts" originated in our minds when they are really his underhanded attempts to weaken us spiritually.

If the thoughts in our minds don't line up with the Word, we need to seriously consider their source. They may well be coming from our own carnal natures, but they may also be coming from the voice of the adversary speaking the lies he began in heavenly places and still tries to promote today ... words of rebellion, words of doubt, words of questioning God's motives.

And I'll just throw this in for free: It's possible to dull our spiritual hearing by listening to words spoken against our leadership. Will your heart be open to your pastor's ministry if you've been listening to people criticize him? Keep your ears free from the pollution of all gossip, but especially against the ministry.

To sum it up, guard the gate of your hearing ... **internally** – by refusing to dwell on thoughts contrary to God's Word, and **externally** – by controlling your environment and the entertainment choices you make.

Dear Jesus, thank You for giving me ears to hear Your Word and Your call on my life. Please help me be aware of the things I allow entrance into my heart through the gateway of hearing. There are so many good choices that would nourish my soul, but there are also a lot of bad options I would do better to avoid. Give me spiritual discernment in the choices I make — choosing to build up instead of tear down or compromise Your call to holy living.

CHAPTER REVIEW AND APPLICATION

The major theme of this chapter is:

_____

_____

How do the things we listen to impact our spirits?

_____

_____

How is our sense of hearing like a radio?

_____

_____

Take a moment to consider the entertainment choices and the voices you have been listening to. Are they pure, lovely and of a good report as Philippians 4:8 instructs?

_____

_____

What does GIGO stand for, and what does it mean?

_____

_____

How does satan's background as a ministering angel of music equip him to use that medium to effectively corrupt our walk with God?

_____

_____

How do "inaudible" words that we hear in our hearts and minds affect our walk with God?

_____

_____

What are some steps you could take to limit the negative influences you hear (audibly and otherwise) and increase the positive influences?

_____

_____

As you purpose to please God by honoring His Word regarding the things you choose to listen to, take a moment to write your personal prayer to Him.

_____

_____

_____

_____

_____

_____

_____

_____

_____

_____

_____

_____

As Christ's ambassadors to the world, we need to be aware of the impact (positive or negative) that our words are having on those around us, even in small ways – like complaining.

12

TALK THE WALK

The Gateway of Spoken Words

We've discussed how the words we hear affect us, but now let's examine the words we say. I hate to admit it, but as soon as I say, "I would never ...." that's when I am often immediately tempted to do that which I have just spoken against. It's like the devil is listening, and he is going to try to snag me with my own words. If I fail, he gets two birds with one stone. Not only do I sin, but I also feel like a gigantic hypocrite, too.

One of my good friends has a sign on her refrigerator that says, "Be careful that your words are sweet, tomorrow you may have to eat them." I know that's true from personal experience. We need to watch how we talk about other people, because Scripture makes it clear we could easily fall into the same temptation (Galatians 6:1).

Truthfulness gets high priority with God. Why does it matter so much? Because God is Truth (John 14:6). It's His very nature.

Honesty must be the foundation for all our relationships. Without that base, there is no real relationship. Besides, God knows what's in our hearts, and He's not willing to compromise on this issue.

That doesn't mean He wants us to be phonies. He's not looking for empty words or lip service. We can be honest with God even in our struggles. However, He demands truth in word and deed in our relationships with Him and with each other. Just read this.

> *But the cowardly, the unbelieving, the vile, the murderers, the sexually immoral, those who practice magic arts, the idolaters and **all liars**—their place will be in the fiery lake of burning sulfur. This is the second death.* (Revelation 21:8 NIV)

Liars keep company with a rough crowd! The Word says that liars go to the pit! You lie, you fry!

Perhaps that seems a little harsh, but here's the heart of the matter. The language we speak reveals our parentage. When we speak the truth, we are speaking the language of our Heavenly Father. When we speak lies, we speak the language of His enemy, the father of lies. Who's your daddy?

> *You belong to your father, the devil, and you want to carry out your father's desire. He was a murderer from the beginning, not holding to the truth, for there is no truth in*

him. When he lies, he speaks his native language, for he is a
liar and the father of lies. (John 8:44 NIV)

The language we speak reveals our parentage. When we speak the truth, we are speaking the language of our Heavenly Father. When we speak lies, we speak the language of His enemy, the father of lies.

Our words are not idle. They live on ... and we can't take them back. Don't you wish you could go back in time and erase some of the things you've said over the years? I know I do.

But I say unto you, That every idle word that men shall speak,
they shall give account thereof in the day of judgment.
(Matthew 12:36)

It's important to keep our language clean and make good choices in the words we use. One vital reason is our witness to the world. If we're at school or on the job and one minute we're talking about what a great church service we had, and the next we're telling a bad joke or swearing because we caught our fingers in the file cabinet, that sends a mixed message to the world we need to reach for Christ.

Can both fresh water and salt water flow from the same spring? My brothers, can a fig tree bear olives, or a grapevine bear figs? Neither can a salt spring produce fresh water. (James 3:11-12 NIV)

I can be pretty impulsive, but there are some things I depend on to be predictable – like the things I'm planning to eat and drink. Recently I brought home about 50 bottles of orange drink for my kids and stuck them in the refrigerator. My daughter had a guest over who took one swig of hers and just about gagged. Somehow, although it hadn't been opened, it had fermented. So gross! It wasn't what she was expecting when she took that drink.

The same concept holds true for what comes out of our mouths. Are the words of our mouths what others expect to hear from a Christian?

Let the words of my mouth, and the meditations of my heart be acceptable in Thy sight, Oh Lord, my strength and my redeemer. (Psalms 19:14)

It should go without saying that verbal filth is unacceptable. If we are using bad language, it's a sad revelation of the condition of our hearts (Matthew 12:34).

But now you must rid yourselves of all such things as these: anger, rage, malice, slander, and filthy language from your lips. (Colossians 3:8 NIV)

Let your speech be always with grace… (Colossians 4:6)

ℒ

We know we shouldn't use profanity. That's a "no-brainer" for a Christian. But what do you think about using "minced oaths?"

That's not a term we use every day, so let's look at its definition. First, what does minced mean? Think about a recipe. When you're making spaghetti sauce, you don't throw a whole bulb of garlic in the pan. You mince it first. That means you cut or chop it into very small pieces. So if you mince the garlic before you put it in the pan, you still have garlic in there, right?

Minced oaths are "softened" expressions based on profanity (usually religious in nature) that have been altered to minimize the objectionable traits of the original terms. However, just like the onion that was still an onion after it was minced, these words are still profane (which means irreverent or vulgar). Due to the very offensive nature of some of these words, we will only go over a few of them.

Thou shalt not take the name of the LORD thy God in vain; for the LORD will not hold him guiltless that taketh his name in vain. (Exodus 20:7)

If we aren't to take God's name in vain, is it okay to take the Name, manipulate it into another form and use that instead? I would think not. Yet, what follows are some alternate words used for Christ, Jesus and God.

Crikey, Gee, Gee whizz, Gee willikers, Gosh, Jeez, Sheesh, Bejeez, Jeepers Creepers, Jiminy Cricket and Judas Priest.

If you wanted to say eternal damnation, there are alternate words here as well:

Dad gummit, G.D., Goldarnit, Dablastit, Dag nabbit, Dang it, Dog gone it, Gosh darn it, Darn it and Heck.

And then there are your generic vulgarisms for body functions:

Crap, Shoot, Sheesh, Suck, Freaking ...

... and that's as far as I'm going.

I didn't provide these words to increase your vocabulary, and this is only a small fraction of a list that came straight from the encyclopedia. It's not some oversensitive lady's interpretation, but the real origins of the words. No matter the reason – if we're mad, trying to make someone laugh, or whatever – we need to watch the language we use.

But among you there must not be even a hint of sexual immorality, or of any kind of impurity, or of greed, because these are improper for God's holy people .Nor should there be obscenity, foolish talk or coarse joking, which are out of place, but rather thanksgiving. For of this you can be sure: No immoral, impure or greedy person—such a man is an idolater—has any inheritance in the kingdom of Christ and of God. Let no one deceive you with empty words, for because of such things God's wrath comes on those who are disobedient. Therefore do not be partners with them. (Ephesians 5:3-7 NIV)

How about this unique idea ... why not use the English language to express your feelings without all the junk words? Anyone can string together a list of low class expletives that don't really convey the message they want to transmit. Use your gift of language well, and think about what you are saying. Is your every day vocabulary God honoring?

As Christ's ambassadors to the world, we need to be aware of the impact (positive or negative) our words have on those around us, even in small ways – like complaining.

Do everything without complaining or arguing, so that you may become blameless and pure, children of God without fault in a crooked and depraved generation, in which you shine like stars in the universe. (Philippians 2:14-15 NIV)

Jesus, please help me pay attention to the language I use no matter where I am or who I am with. My words can build up or tear down, nourish or annihilate. Set a watch before my mouth and keep the gate of my lips. You are serious about lying, gossiping complaining and profanity. You have a record of every idle word I've spoken. Forgive me for the inappropriate conversations I've had, and fill my mouth with good things like thanksgiving, praise and encouragement so I can be a light in this world.

CHAPTER REVIEW AND APPLICATION

The major theme of this chapter is:

_____

_____

Why do you think truthfulness is so important to God?

_____

_____

Does truthfulness affect the quality of your relationships with your friends and family members?

_____

_____

How does the language we use affect our Christian witness?

_____

_____

_____

As it relates to your conversation, what do you think the Bible means by: *"Can both fresh water and salt water flow from the same spring?"*

_____

_____

What is a "minced oath?"

_____

_____

Do you think it's okay to dilute a profane word and use it in a different format? Why?

_____

_____

_____

How do you think exaggeration and our desire to insert emotional impact in our conversation affect our use of minced oaths, and is this acceptable?

_____

_____

_____

As you purpose to please God by obeying His Word in the language you use, take a moment to write your personal prayer to Him.

_____

_____

_____

_____

_____

_____

_____

_____

_____

_____

_____

_____

When the Word says, "Abhor that which is evil; cleave to that which is good" (Romans 12:9), we know we must apply this to every area of our lives, including the things we put before our eyes.

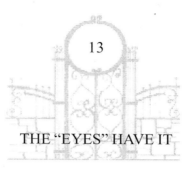

13

THE "EYES" HAVE IT

The Gateway of Vision

Our eyes are visual gateways into our minds and spirits. Have you ever thought about how they actually work? Our eyes can't receive images without processing light. To view an object, light must first enter the cornea, go through the pupil, through the iris, through the lens, and through five more steps before it even hits the brain for processing! Isn't that amazing!

Without the light properly interacting with the visual organ of the eye, natural blindness occurs. We can live in spiritual blindness as well, if we aren't interacting with the "Light" for our souls. This, of course, is the Light of God revealed to mankind in the life of Jesus Christ (John 1:1-14).

Did you know that God has His eye on you? We live our lives in the sight of the Lord.

Behold, the eye of the LORD is upon them that fear Him, upon them that hope in His mercy. (Psalm 33:18)

The eyes of the LORD are in every place, beholding the evil and the good. (Proverbs 15:3)

Zechariah 2:8 says we are the apple of God's eye! And He's got us covered from every angle. We're glad for God's attentiveness when we think of His protection and provision, but there may be times we'd prefer He wasn't watching. After all, He's seeing everything we're seeing … and He's given some clear instructions on what we should be focusing on and what we should be steering away from.

The eye is the lamp of the body. If your eyes are good, your whole body will be full of light. But if your eyes are bad, your whole body will be full of darkness. If then the light within you is darkness, how great is that darkness! (Matthew 6:22-23 NIV)

When we look at the concept of light and darkness and how it compares to vision and blindness, this verse takes on new meaning. We can't see spiritual things outside of the Light of God. He connects us to the spiritual by being the Light in our world. In the natural, light enables the eye to discern form and color. In the spiritual, God enables our spirits to see – to see the things we might bump into in the darkness – to see the pits that may be in our pathway – to see the beauty of the grace of God and the hope of our salvation.

$$\mathcal{D}$$

A 16th Century Yiddish proverb says, "Our eyes are the mirrors of our souls." What we focus on reflects what's in our hearts. The reverse is also true. People can see something of our character when they look into our eyes.

The Bible talks about all kinds of eyes: scornful, adulterous, tender, dim, blind, evil, enlightened, mourning, lofty, bountiful, dove's, wanton, pure, heavy, blessed, understanding, and lustful. The eyes reveal the *intent* and *character* of the person to whom they belong, as well as what they are focusing on – good or bad.

We've discussed fleeing from temptation, but this is the appropriate place to talk about how the things we look at can lead us down a path we don't want to walk on. One example in Scripture is the story of King David and Bathsheba. David was wandering around on his rooftop when his eyes landed upon a beautiful woman washing herself. David knew who she was, her name, even her husband and father ... but the more he looked, the more he had to have her. And so he did, which resulted in serious consequences, including the murderous death of Bathsheba's husband. David could have turned away when he discovered Bathsheba bathing and spared a lot of people a lot of pain.

And it's not just the guys! Women can be just as guilty. Potiphar's wife "cast her eyes upon Joseph" causing all sorts of problems for him.

Of course, we can't help running into things we shouldn't look at in our world today. But what we can control is how we respond. Will we choose to dwell on the ungodly, or will we turn away from it?

Then said I unto them, Cast ye away every man the abominations of his eyes, and defile not yourselves... (Ezekiel 20:7)

Turn my eyes away from worthless things; preserve my life according to your word. (Psalm 119:37 NIV)

The Bible doesn't give us a complete list of "DOs and DON'Ts," but it does provide principles and guidelines to follow. When the Word says "Abhor that which is evil; cleave to that which is good" (Romans 12:9), we know that we must apply this to every area of our lives, including the things we put before our eyes.

Although it doesn't spell out "thou shalt not watch MTV and rated R movies," we are still accountable to the principle of holiness in the Bible. And it's more than just the station and the rating we need to look at. It's also the content. If we are watching things that glorify sin in any fashion, we are lifting up that sin in our lives. God is the One who deserves to be lifted up, not sin.

> *If we are watching things that glorify sin in any fashion, we are lifting up that sin in our lives. God is the One who deserves to be lifted up, not sin.*

What benefit could we possibly gain from watching shows depicting others participating in sinful activities and conversations? In doing so, we participate in these forbidden practices in our minds and emotions and promote the desire to join in affairs that separate us from God.

I hope we don't need to cover the fact that viewing pornographic material is a form of sexual sin. We do need to be alert, however, to the "soft porn" that comes in the form of catalogs and brochures right to our own mailboxes. Some of the catalogs specifically geared toward teenagers not only feature partial nudity and immodest clothing, but they actually go so far as to promote homosexuality. I pray that we will consider the "image" we are identifying with and the companies we are supporting when we purchase from these retailers – especially when their labels are plastered across the fronts or backs of our t-shirts and we are their walking billboards!

Test everything. Hold on to the good. Avoid every kind of evil.
(I Thessalonians 5:21-22)

And have no fellowship with the unfruitful works of darkness, but rather reprove them. (Ephesians 5:11)

$\mathscr{D}$

God has gifted us all in different ways, and we are all at different stages of development and maturity in our talents and spiritual walks. That's why we need to be cautious of watching others and comparing ourselves to them. There will always be someone "worse" than me, so I can attempt to justify my sin. There will always be someone "better" so I feel like I fall short. What *I* need to keep focused on is *my* calling and growth, and *you* need to focus on *yours*.

They measuring themselves by themselves, and comparing themselves among themselves, are not wise. (II Corinthians 10:12)

And I'll just throw this in for free, because it really "caught my eye!"

The eye that mocks a father, that scorns obedience to a mother, will be pecked out by the ravens of the valley, will be eaten by the vultures. (Proverbs 30:17 NIV)

But let's end our study on an encouraging word:

"But as it is written, Eye hath not seen, nor ear heard, neither have entered into the heart of man, the things which God hath prepared for them that love him." (I Corinthians 2:9)

We have a bright and beautiful future when we serve the Lord! Better than we can even imagine!

Lord, Your Word cautions me to be wise in the things I set before my eyes. You knew I'd want whatever I focused on – whether good or bad. I pray You would cleanse my mind from the things I've unwisely chosen to watch in the past and help me in the future to turn away from anything that would weaken my faith in You or put ungodly desires in my heart.

Jesus, You're worth it all. You've opened my eyes through this book and by Your Holy Spirit to see areas in my life where I need to apply Your Word and develop a more Christ-like nature. I know You are forgiving — a God of restoration — and it's Your desire to draw each person closer to You. I pray that in the areas where I've "gotten it wrong," You will show me the way to make it right from here. There's nothing I've done that isn't redeemable through Your sacrificial gift of grace and mercy on the cross.

In my human weakness, I know I will always be dependant upon You. I place my faith in You again today. Forgive me. Cleanse me. Clothe me in Your righteousness. And keep me safe inside the gates and fences You established for my blessing and protection.

In Jesus' Name, Amen.

CHAPTER REVIEW AND APPLICATION

The major theme of this chapter is:

_____

_____

How does the visual organ of the eye depend on light to work?

_____

_____

How does the Light of God's Spirit in Christ Jesus and the written Word affect our spiritual vision?

_____

_____

What do you think Scripture means when it says for your eye to "be good?"

_____

_____

How did King David's decision to keep looking at Bathsheba lead him into sin?

_____

_____

Do you think things could have worked out differently if he had chosen to look away and think on something else ... like his own wife?

_____

_____

Although the Bible doesn't specifically mention things like MTV and rated R movies, do you think that the principles in the Word of God apply to watching these things? Why or why not?

_____

_____

How is watching immoral shows and behaviors having fellowship with the unfruitful works of darkness (Ephesians 5:11)?

_____

_____

As you purpose to please God by obeying His Word in the things you choose to watch, take a moment to write your personal prayer to Him.

_____

_____

_____

_____

_____

_____

_____

_____

_____

_____

_____

_____

Chapter 1
http://www.christiananswers.net/dictionary/rome.html

Chapter 4
Hammond, Colleen. Dressing with Dignity. TAN Books & Publishers, Inc., © 2005

Henry, Matthew A. Matthew Henry's Commentary on the Whole Bible. Hendrickson Publishers © 1990

Chapter 6
Journal of Adolescent Research, Vol. 1, No. 3, 361-371 (1986). SAGE Publications © 1986

Harris, Joshua. I Kissed Dating Goodbye. Multnomah Publishers © 1999, 2003

Holy Bible. New Living Translation. Tyndale Charitable Trust © 1996, 2004

Chapter 7
http://en.wikipedia.org/wiki/Paradise_garden

Chapter 8
http://en.wikipedia.org/wiki/Truth_or_Consequences

http://www.parentspromotinginnocence.org/overviewofcommonstds.html

Chapter 9
Vine, W.E., Vine's Expository Dictionary of New Testament Words. Published without copyright in 1940

Chapter 12
http://en.wikipedia.org/wiki/Gosh

Chapter 13
http://www.pixi.com/~gedwards/eyes/eyeanat.html

ADDITIONAL RESOURCES

www.biblegateway.com
www.dictionary.com

PHOTO CREDITS

Christina Harper: Pages 4, 31, 43, 63, 73, 83, 101, 111, 123, 137, front and back covers
Lori Wagner: Pages 11, 21, 53
Noelle Wagner-Kalajian: Pages 93, 167

*May you enjoy the
pure freedom that comes
from obedience to the Word
... living safely inside the
protection and blessings of
God's best plans
for your life!*

The Bill Wagner Family
November 2005

For information on bulk purchases of *Gates and Fences* or to
schedule Lori Wagner for a speaking engagement, contact:

Affirming Faith
1181 Whispering Knoll Lane
Rochester Hills, MI 48306
(248) 909-5735
loriwagner@affirmingfaith.com
www.affirmingfaith.com

Affirming Faith is pleased to announce Lori Wagner's new book
Quilting Patches of Life scheduled for release October 2007.